MOMENTS WITH ONESELF SERIES: 5

FUNDAMENTAL PROBLEM

SWAMI DAYANANDA SARASWATI

ARSHA VIDYA

ARSHA VIDYA
RESEARCH AND PUBLICATION TRUST
CHENNAI

Published by :
Arsha Vidya Research
and Publication Trust
32 / 4 ' Sri Nidhi ' Apts III Floor
Sir Desika Road Mylapore
Chennai 600 004 INDIA
Tel   : 044 2499 7023
Telefax: 2499 7131
Email   : avrandpc@gmail.com

ISBN : 978 - 81 - 904203 - 0 - 3

Revised Edition : August   2007   Copies : 2000
1st Reprint   : November   2009   Copies : 2000

Design :
Suchi Ebrahim

Printed by :
Sudarsan Graphics
27, Neelakanta Mehta Street
T. Nagar, Chennai 600 017
Email : info@sudarsan.com

CONTENTS

KEY TO TRANSLITERATION AND PRONUNCIATION OF
SANSKRIT LETTERS

Sanskrit is a highly phonetic language and hence accuracy in articulation of the letters is important. For those unfamiliar with the *Devanāgari* script, the international transliteration is a guide to the proper pronunciation of Sanskrit letters.

अ	*a*	(b*u*t)	ट	*ṭa*	(*t*rue)*3
आ	*ā*	(f*a*ther)	ठ	*ṭha*	(an*th*ill)*3
इ	*i*	(*i*t)	ड	*ḍa*	(*d*rum)*3
ई	*ī*	(b*ea*t)	ढ	*ḍha*	(go*dh*ead)*3
उ	*u*	(f*u*ll)	ण	*ṇa*	(u*n*der)*3
ऊ	*ū*	(p*oo*l)	त	*ta*	(pa*th*)*4
ऋ	*ṛ*	(*rh*ythm)	थ	*tha*	(*th*under)*4
ॠ	*ṝ*	(ma*ri*ne)	द	*da*	(*th*at)*4
ऌ	*ḷ*	(reve*lry*)	ध	*dha*	(brea*the*)*4
ए	*e*	(pl*ay*)	न	*na*	(*n*ut)*4
ऐ	*ai*	(*ai*sle)	प	*pa*	(*p*ut) 5
ओ	*o*	(g*o*)	फ	*pha*	(loo*ph*ole)*5
औ	*au*	(l*ou*d)	ब	*ba*	(*b*in) 5
क	*ka*	(see*k*) 1	भ	*bha*	(a*bh*or)*5
ख	*kha*	(bloc*kh*ead)*1	म	*ma*	(*m*uch) 5
ग	*ga*	(*g*et) 1	य	*ya*	(lo*y*al)
घ	*gha*	(lo*g h*ut)*1	र	*ra*	(*r*ed)
ङ	*ṅa*	(si*ng*) 1	ल	*la*	(*l*uck)
च	*ca*	(*ch*unk) 2	व	*va*	(*v*ase)
छ	*cha*	(cat*ch h*im)*2	श	*śa*	(*s*ure)
ज	*ja*	(*j*ump) 2	ष	*ṣa*	(*sh*un)
झ	*jha*	(he*dg*ehog)*2	स	*sa*	(*s*o)
ञ	*ña*	(bu*n*ch) 2	ह	*ha*	(*h*um)

•	ṁ	*anusvāra*	(nasalisation of preceding vowel)
:	ḥ	*visarga*	(aspiration of preceding vowel)
*			No exact English equivalents for these letters

1.	Guttural	–	Pronounced from throat
2.	Palatal	–	Pronounced from palate
3.	Lingual	–	Pronounced from cerebrum
4.	Dental	–	Pronounced from teeth
5.	Labial	–	Pronounced from lips

The 5th letter of each of the above class – called nasals – are also pronounced nasally.

A *mumukṣu* is one who discerns the basic human problem of self-non-acceptance and seeks freedom from this. It is from this standpoint that Vedanta helps us start the inquiry.

All our problems of seeking originate in the mind. When we are in deep sleep, we are not conscious of any struggle. But when we are awake we are constantly challenged by thoughts and situations. Our urge is to resolve all disturbances and bring about certain order both within and without. The human mind has this capacity to inquire into the nature and meaning of things, to reason out, to analyse, to come to conclusions and make choices.

An animal is programmed to live its life, governed by its inborn instinct and the urge to survive. For instance, a cow instinctively fulfils the need to nourish its body by eating grass. It does not deliberate to be a vegetarian nor does it insist that the only way to enjoy the grass is with a special gourmet sauce. The instincts allow the animal to sustain its life. Consequently the urge for survival is its attraction to that which supports and enhances its survival and its retreat from that which is painful or which threatens its survival.

Similarly, a human being wants his or her body with its various systems to survive and function without pain, disease and decline. These natural urges must be fulfilled so that the system can continue to thrive. Whatever is born moves naturally towards sustaining its life and away from terminating it. A human being, however, has an intellect, a thinking faculty and hence mere bodily survival does not make his or her life. He or she not only wants to continue living but to live in a particular way.

If we naturally seek to sustain our life, we also seek to fulfil the natural urges of the mind. The mind, being an instrument of reason, seeks certain modicum of clarity. It moves, shifts and changes, wanting to shed ignorance and confusion. It wants to feel at ease with its thoughts and moods, thus, wanting to be at home in its environment. This makes the human mind self-aware and self-conscious. Being aware of ourselves, we cannot but be a desirer, a seeker. It means the very essence of our life is that we are after ends. They may be lofty, profound or profane.

What I really want is to be free from want. That 'I want' is exactly what I do not want. To fulfil a desire is actually to get rid of it. Therefore, to say 'I want' is really to say that I do not want to have any want. Yet I cannot help but want, for being self-conscious I am conscious of my incompleteness. If I do not take myself to be incomplete, I would not want to be different from what I am. The sense of incompleteness expresses itself through the seeking of different ends. It is not something I cultivate or learn in time. An infant also has wants. It may not know exactly what it wants, but in addition to merely wanting to live, it also wants that which will make it feel good, happy, secure and so on. As we grow, our desires become defined, refined and constantly renovated according to our cultivated likes and dislikes, ethics, values, whims and moods at a given moment.

Thus, we find that in addition to the basic urge to survive, there seems to be another basic urge to have things go well with us which manifests in the mind as: 'I want to be full, complete, adequate, fulfilled and happy.' In whichever way we say, it amounts to the same thing. Unlike all the cultivated desires for specific ends that we pick up in time, this one seems to come along with birth. It is a desire that our forefathers also had. No one has to be told that being full and happy is a desirable thing.

In order to satisfy that urge, I seek something, be it an object, a situation, a person and so on, believing or hoping that a change in a given condition will result in, or bring me closer to the full person I want to be. A water buffalo does not desire to live in Brooklyn or go to the Himalayas for vacation, muchless it wants to change its hairstyle or become a cow! But a human being always wants to change some aspect of his or her situation. I am painfully aware of my incompleteness and cannot stand it. The urge to be full and complete is not a peculiar trait of some particular person; it is common to all human beings of all times. It is implicit in any action that extends beyond mere instinctual bodily survival. It is, in fact, the desire behind all topical desires, the fundamental desire, the mother desire, for it is the desire that gives birth to all desires and motivations.

I choose to dress in a particular way, buy a summer house, get a better job, have a meaningful relationship, rid myself of bad habits and so on. The reason is that it is not for the sake of the thing itself but for my own sake, for the feeling it invokes in me when I gain it.

It is important to see, to understand this clearly, for this is the end we are really after.

Having determined the end we should now be able to arrive at the appropriate and adequate means to achieve that end. First, however, let us see what it means when we say we want to be complete, full, and adequate. The experience of happiness is known to all of us. Since it is known, we seek and struggle for it all through our life.

When I am happy at a particular time, I feel free of all limitations; I am myself. It is that self I love to be, live to be, I seek to be in all my desired ends. Is completeness, that I seek, something limited, something relative? If what I am seeking is actually a specific object, then I am, in fact, seeking a limited end, for all objects are limited in time and space. The completeness I seek cannot be limited because whatever is limited is dependent on factors other than itself for its sustenance, and is therefore incomplete. At the present moment, I am dependent upon a number of things and situations for the sense of my well-being. It is this very dependency that gives me a sense of incompleteness. What I want is freedom from dependency because, otherwise, my well-being is at the mercy of conditions that are themselves subject to change based on yet other conditions.

Behind all my seeking and struggles, if what I actually sought were only another state, like the one that obtains at present, then every pursuit would become meaningless.

Completeness is not a measurable entity. It is not a finite quantity that I keep adding things to myself and one day I become full and complete. It is like saying 1000 units of achievements will make me full but subtract one and I become incomplete. Such thinking is fallacious; neither is that fullness within the realm of experience, for I find that a person with name, fame and fortune is not necessarily a fulfilled person. In fact, I find such persons seeking even more than others.

If, in every desire, what I really want is to put an end to the wanting person, it is clear that the wanting person will not go unless the person is already complete, limitless and lacking nothing. Only then can I be contented. If this is true, is it realistic and reasonable to say that I want to be free from want? It is. What I find is, no matter what the gain be, no matter how rewarding it be for the time being, I do not cease being a seeker, a desirer of ends. No end satisfies or can satisfy that urge for completeness. In fact, the expression 'that's life' commiserates with the reality built into the nature of every gain that makes it fall short of its intended mark. I either laugh or weep at that fact and go on to the next pursuit in the hope that it will bring me closer to the real end.

In addition to the impermanence of acquired ends is the fact that my values, my moods are constantly changing. So the one who receives the sought after end is not exactly the one who sought it. Thus, even the impact of the gain loses its potency or meaning, since the gain itself is limited. For every gain there is always a price, a loss. If nothing else, there is the loss of its prior condition. Even as I read these pages, I lose the opportunity to watch the television, which may be equally appealing. I have to choose. Under no circumstances can I physically be here and also there at the same time. Any choice necessarily involves negation, and, or elimination, while I always hope I have chosen the better alternative. But all that I find in the world is only limited ends.

What we have discerned, both logically and experientially, is that we seek in our heart to be free of limitation; we want an end that does not come to an end. Perhaps we do not know the nature of such an end because we do not seem to have employed the proper means. Can there be a means that would result in a limitless end? For gaining the ends we have not yet achieved, there is a spectrum of means available in the world. Between an end to be accomplished and the one who wants to accomplish it, there is always a distance, a gap in terms of time and space. To bridge that gap we must put forth the proper effort, be it physical or mental. But then, what we can produce by effort will always be limited, because the very effort itself is limited.

An action cannot produce a result that is not inherent therein. I cannot walk lying down. An action can only produce a result that is appropriate to that action. So, by the very laws inherent in any action I find that what I gain in the world is limited, but what I seek is limitless. It is a 'Catch 22' situation. It is logical. I am limited and I go after something that is limited, through limited means. Insecure plus insecure, being bound by time, the result is insecure. Incomplete plus one million equals the same, incomplete because it is logical and it is also my experience. A finite sum like one and another finite sum like one million are both equally away from infinity. So, in discovering the end that I really seek,

I have arrived at the problem I am facing. The problem is that I cannot help but seek completeness, yet there is nothing available by which I can gain it.

This is recognised by a *mumukṣu*. A sense of despair may prevail upon this realisation. However, it is not a state of self-condemnation but of self-appreciation, for that is the nature of the solution. I cannot give up the urge for completeness, happiness. It is what makes it **the fundamental problem**.

The problem is natural and what is natural should be meaningful. As a natural urge, the desire to be limitless must have a solution just as other natural urges, such as hunger and thirst have. Whatever is natural about the self is always gladly accepted. For instance, I do not complain that the eyes see. I am not irritated because there are eyeballs in the eye sockets. But if there is a small speck of dust in the eye, I cannot stand it. Even the physiological system cannot accept those bugs that do not belong to the system. In fact, a battle rages within the body with shooting temperatures because the intruders have to be rejected. So too, I do not want to remain inadequate, unhappy and incomplete. These are conditions the mind cannot accept. I want to shake them off because they are intruders; they are unnatural. Since my nature is the opposite of what I cannot stand, it is natural for me to be without them; I try to get rid of them as fast as I can.

If I cannot stand sorrow and agitation, my nature must be happiness and peacefulness. Otherwise why should I not stand sorrow? I should be quite at home with sorrow, if it is my nature. Since I am not, it is obvious that sorrow is not natural to me. Consequently, all I seek is my own nature. The happiness, the peace of mind that I seek is what I am. If it is so, then why do I miss it? I cannot miss myself. Yet if I keep missing and searching for it, through countless plans and schemes, doing endless things, the search obviously stems from self-disowning and self-ignorance.

The problem is now clear. It is a problem that is different from ordinary problems, for the end is of a different nature. What I want to gain is not something away from me, not something different from me and not something yet to be achieved. What I want to gain is what I want to be. What I want is myself. The means for this end must differ from just putting forth effort, however great the effort may be.

If either going after or going away from something is not involved, does it mean that I can be complete without actions, without becoming? Yes, but the word 'become' has no meaning here, for every becoming involves a change and a change involves a loss. If, without a change, I am to 'become' complete, then clearly it must be the gain of the already gained. It is precisely because of the apparent paradox of the problem, the search appears to be shrouded in mystery. What I seek is hidden in the most secretive place; it is in the very seeker. In the act of seeking I deny the sought, for what I seek is different from me.

If what I seek is already with me, obviously I am ignorant of the fact. The only recourse for me is to know that I already have what I seek. For instance, I search for my spectacles, the very same pair that I have absentmindedly placed over my head. I go around searching for them, while all the time they are with me. All efforts are in vain. I simply do not know that I already own them. It is knowledge that will make me the possessor of the glasses. The seeker, that is I, and the sought, the possessor of the spectacles, are one and the same. The problem, therefore, being one of ignorance, can be resolved only by knowledge. If there is self-disownment and self-ignorance, there must also be self-knowledge. It is this knowledge that a *mumukṣu* seeks. It is Vedanta.

When we talk of self-knowledge, we have to determine what that self is, the meaning of 'I am'. What do we mean when we say 'I'? It is ironical that the word 'I' which we use constantly throughout the day and from the standpoint of which we view and judge the world, has no definite object in our mind.

Any word I use elicits an external object or concept in the mind. I utter the word 'pot' and a thought-form corresponding to the object pot occurs. This is the basis of all communication. If I hear the word 'pot' and see instead a cot, then my knowledge is erroneous. If I see nothing, I would say, I am totally ignorant of the object 'pot'. For instance, I say '*gagabugain*' a meaningless group of syllables; it definitely does not connote something specific. Every word has a corresponding object. But when I say 'I' hundreds of times in a day, who is this 'I'? Who is this 'I' that I experience so intimately? For, it seems it is this 'I' that is unhappy, which cannot get its life together. It is this 'I' which wants to fulfil its potential, its capacities, and which wants a meaningful relationship, which does not want to suffer. It is this 'I' that wants to know himself or herself. I want to address this 'I'; I want to see this 'I'.

Who is this 'I'? When I inquire into the nature of 'I,' it is clear the 'I' is a conscious being and that everything other than 'I,' is the world.

We can reduce the entire creation into two factors. One is the subject and the other, the object. Anything I can objectify is the object and I, the one who objectifies am the subject. In an object, I do not have the 'I' notion, the 'I' sense. I am not where the object is because it is something I know. 'I' is always the subject. An object need not always be tangible. There are intangible things I appreciate and know. I am aware of time and space, for example, which are not tangible but are still objects of my knowledge.

Although it is quite clear that 'I' is the subject, since the subject is distinct from any object of knowledge, still I tend to conclude that the physical body is I, the subject. It is everyone's intimate experience that 'I' is confined to the extremities of the body and the world exists outside its boundaries. I do not exist, for example, in the space between my fingers, whereas there is certainly no remoteness from feeling the pain even if it is in a corner of the body. When my toe is hurt, I am hurt. I know my body with all its corners and crevices. However, I tend to overlook the fact that the physical body is an object of knowledge not only for me, but for others too.

It is obvious now the subject and the object are two distinct, separate entities. The knower of a thing is distinct from the thing he or she knows. From this I understand that I cannot be the physical body. Similarly, I cannot attribute the identity of 'I' to any function or system of the body, because it involves the same subject-object, knower-known relationship. For instance, I know my sense organs as well as their functions. When I say that I am blind, it is with reference to my eyes; I am short or tall with reference to my physical body; I am hungry with reference to the physiological condition. Further, I am an uncle, cousin, mother and so on with reference to different people. I, the subject, however, am neither of these nor a composite of these. In each case I am looking at myself from a particular standpoint which can be objectified.

Every situation, from moment to moment, invokes in me a person relevant to that situation. For instance, when I see my son, I am father. It is this relative 'I' that I confront all the time. It is this relative 'I' that has all the problems. 'I' as a daughter has a problem; 'I' as a short person has a problem. Never do I confront the absolute 'I' that is present in all these relative roles. It means, if there is an absolute I, a central I, as such, there is no occasion when that 'I' is known.

When I commit an error, taking myself to be other than the complete self, that error cannot help me. On the contrary, I lose in this transaction. The 'I' is free from any limitation, but I have concluded that I am the body, taking on to myself all its limitations. If I am neither the physical body, nor the sense organs, nor the physiological system, nor any relative role I play, then what is 'I'? Perhaps I am the mind. But, what do I mean when I say mind? I cannot take myself as the tangible brain. The brain itself is an object, as are the functions of the brain. I know, I am aware of the thoughts and emotions such as perception, inference, conclusion, doubts, restlessness, depression, agitation and so on.

Furthermore, any one thought cannot be 'I' because, despite the thought moving and changing, the 'I' remains. So, when I say, 'I am restless or agitated,' I am speaking only of the conditions of the mind. I am not the mind, for I am the one who is aware of all thoughts. The thoughts come and go but I remain. Before the thought arrives, while the thought is and even after it goes away, I am very much present.

It means I am independent of thought. In Sanskrit we call the mind, with its various functions, as *antaḥkaraṇa*. *Karaṇa* means an instrument. So, the mind is an instrument capable of giving me knowledge, imagination, memories, emotions and problems. Being an instrument, it has to be in the hands of someone different from it, like any other instrument; for example the telescope does not see through itself; it requires a subject, a seer. Therefore, 'I' cannot be the mind. Perhaps I could say, 'I am ignorance.' It is different from all these. But I also know ignorance. What I know, I know and what I do not know also I know. For instance, I know that I do not know Russian language.

Consequently, if I analyse I would have to just say, I am...I am... I am, I exist and I know. I am but a knower of various things. The things I know vary but I am the one who knows all the time. Here we need to go one more step. If I am the knower of all these, I am the knower only when there is something to know, that is with reference to things known, I am the knower. If I reduce the identity of 'I' to knower, what does 'knower' mean? It means the one who is aware of. I am the awarer. The awarer and knower are functional words. The suffix 'er' is added with reference to a function such as driver, speaker, runner and so on. It denotes the one who does something and it is a relative term. However, the 'I' that I wish to know is the one who is consciousness, unrelated to anyone or anything. Consciousness can only be the content of the knower. This unqualified consciousness is the meaning of the word 'I'. If I place the 'I' anywhere other than in the subject, the ultimate subject that is consciousness, I will be committing a mistake.

In the body, consciousness is. In the thought, consciousness is. Both depend on consciousness, but consciousness is independent of both. Consciousness depends on nothing. It is self-evident existence; I know I am. Once I see that I am consciousness which is independent, whereas all thoughts and objects are dependent thereof, I am free from all possible limitations that I can ever suffer from.

Vedanta teaches that the self is of the nature of *ānanda*, which means fullness. If the self is pure consciousness, formless, having no characteristics to circumscribe it, it is free from all limitations. It is the very fullness, the very happiness that I seek. It must be clear that the fullness is not the quality of an object outside, nor is it somewhere inside the physical body. Since happiness often coincides with the gain of a desired end or condition, I attribute it to the end or condition. The fact is, at the moment of happiness the mind is not wanting or projecting. It is a wonderful moment because I am just with myself. The happiness, fullness that seem to come and go, which depends on various conditions, is really present all the time as the nature of myself. I am always that fullness but because of ignorance about myself I take myself to be other than what I am.

The self is *sat*, which always is, and which cannot be negated. *Cit*, consciousness, is also *ānanda*, fullness. Just as the clouds cover the sun, ignorance covers the truth about myself. The sun does not change or cease shining but appears other than what it is when covered by clouds.

We showed in the beginning that all human urges and pursuits thereupon, if reduced to their fundamental forms, would be expressed in the desire to live and live happily and to be free from ignorance. When the teaching unfolds, the nature of the self is revealed as:

Sat - existence that can never be negated,

Cit - consciousness and

Ānanda - fullness; without any limit.

It is ironic that given the true nature of the self, we seek happiness elsewhere.

If consciousness is the real meaning of 'I' then this 'I' is no more a historical person. All the problems I suffer from belong to the historical I, the relative I, the 'I' that is falsely identified with the role I play at any given moment. It is like an actor who plays the role of a beggar on stage but takes home the hunger and the poverty of the beggar with him after the show.

Further, when I say, I am restless, I am depressed, I am fat, I am lean and so on, well, they are problems or situations which are objects of my knowledge and not to the subject who witnesses them. It is like watching a congested traffic scene and saying that 'I am congested.' I do watch the traffic-flow of my thoughts but take its various conditions as belonging to the self. It is true, the mind is agitated and the body is fat. These problems belong to the mind and the body and not to I, the subject. This knowledge puts my immediate problems in proper perspective. The problems belong to the object and not to the subject. This is objectivity.

A wise person, knowing himself or herself to be full and complete, is always full and complete in spite of his or her situation. The person is not dependent on a situation or a thing or a condition to be full. A wise person is one who is a master of himself or herself because the person knows the truth of the self.

When I know the truth of the self, I naturally come to know the truth of the world, of the objects of my knowledge. The problem that I originally mistook as being real, and therefore there was a dire need of resolving, I now see as belonging to a false entity. I know that I am the one who gives reality to the entity. I have no problem, for I am full and complete; nothing can add anything to me nor can take anything from me. It is seeing the self and my life as they are. Only then can a topical problem be tackled for what it is. There is total release in this knowledge, for I am no longer a creature in the world.

Vedanta has always been an oral tradition of teaching, passed from teacher to student. It is said to be a *pramāṇa*, that which is instrumental in giving rise to knowledge. Those who come to it as serious dedicated students take it to be a means of knowledge, like even the eyes that are a means of knowledge for knowing colour and form of a physical object. Here, two things are involved, the teacher and the student. Being an oral tradition, it requires a teacher who handles the words, unlocks the meaning behind the words. To say that you are full and limitless is one thing; to make you see what it actually means, is another. If it is not done, the words just create another conditioning.

There is a need for this methodology and it rests in the very nature of the subject matter. What I want to know is what I want to be and it is what I am. The 'I' cannot be objectified and therefore it is not available for any known means of knowledge. All available means of knowledge, be it perception, presumption, inference or illustration, involve some sensory data. The only means of knowledge which has the scope to reveal the self, is the word. But even the word, producing thoughts in the mind, reveals but an object that is different from the subject. The gain of any knowledge necessarily takes place in the mind. However, anything that can be objectified by the mind is other than the subject. Furthermore, what is available for me to communicate with are known words, and they can only produce knowledge of that which is known. If I say, "You are that Brahman," the meaning of the word 'Brahman' is unknown to you. So, I say Brahman means limitless. The word 'limitless' has no co-relative object in the known world. Thus, all I can really communicate is a vague notion or a subjective concept or whatever you take the word to mean.

Consequently, the self is neither an object nor a concept, yet undeniably present. Therefore, the communication of it requires extraordinary handling of words. Words must be elaborately defined so that what is meant by the teacher is what is received by the student. Paradoxes must be juggled, illustrations handled, contexts set up so that the implied meaning of words can be seen. For this, a teacher who knows the truth as well as the methodology for revealing it, is necessary.

Secondly, the one who comes to learn this knowledge comes to it with a particular attitude. Being a *mumukṣu* he has discerned, to a degree, the nature of the problem and so there is receptivity, openness to what the teacher teaches. What is being taught is not the solution to a relative problem; not the opinion of one person, which may or may not be confirmed by additional information; not a speculative philosophy or a system or a school of thought, which may be usurped at a later date by a greater intellect. What is taught is very simply the truth. This really distinguishes self-knowledge from all other types of learning and problem solving. I find that in the very learning process there is love and trust that comes from the relief of discovering the means to what I really want to gain. The teacher is not an authority but is more akin to a candle that is going to light another candle.

Self-knowledge gives us the end that we are seeking in all our pursuits. It solves the fundamental problem, in the sense, the true nature of the owner, the one who is the problem, and the true nature of the problem itself is seen.

Oṁ tat sat

Books by Swami Dayananda Saraswati

Public Talk Series :

1. Living Intelligently
2. Successful Living
3. Need for Cognitive Change
4. Discovering Love
5. Value of Values
6. Vedic View and Way of Life

Upaniṣad Series :

7. Muṇḍakopaniṣad
8. Kenopaniṣad

Text Translation Series :

9. Śrīmad Bhagavad Gītā

   (Text with roman transliteration and English translation)

10. Śrī Rudram

    (Text in Sanskrit with transliteration, word-to-word and verse meaning along with an elaborate commentary in English)

Stotra Series :

11. Dīpārādhanā

12. Prayer Guide

    (With explanations of several Mantras, Stotras, Kirtans and Religious Festivals)

Essays :

Exploring Vedanta Series : (*vākyavicāra*)

Books by Pujya Swamiji's disciples :

Sadhvi Varadaa Caitanya

Dr. Carol Whitfield

Books by Smt. Sheela Balaji :

43. Salutations to Rudra
   (based on the exposition of Śrī Rudram by
   Swami Dayananda Saraswati)

44. Without a Second

Also available at :

ARSHA VIDYA RESEARCH
AND PUBLICATION TRUST
32/4 Sir Desika Road
Mylapore Chennai 600 004
Telefax   : 044 - 2499 7131
Email   : avrandpc@gmail.com

ARSHA VIDYA GURUKULAM
Anaikatti P.O.
Coimbatore 641 108
Ph   : 0422 - 2657001
Fax   : 0422 - 2657002
Email   : office@arshavidya.in

ARSHA VIDYA GURUKULAM
P.O.Box 1059. Pennsylvania
PA 18353, USA.
Ph   : 001-570-992-2339
Email   : avp@epix.net

SWAMI DAYANANDA ASHRAM
Purani Jhadi, P.B. No. 30
Rishikesh, Uttaranchal 249 201
Telefax : 0135-2430769
Email   : ashrambookstore@yahoo.com

AND IN ALL THE LEADING BOOK STORES, INDIA